Work from Anywhere: The Ultimate Guide to Digital Nomadism

Table of Contents

Chapter 1: The **Allure of Digital Nomadism: Freedom, Adventure, and Beyond**

Digital Nomadism—a concept, a lifestyle, a revolution in the traditional view of what it means to work and live. Its resonance has been felt far and wide, especially among those who yearn for a life less ordinary. This first chapter will be an exploration of this phenomenon and its irresistible allure.

The core appeal of digital nomadism lies in its promise of freedom, a value deeply ingrained in our collective consciousness. We all seek freedom in one form or another—the freedom to be who we are, to go where we please, to shape our destinies, and to do what we love. Digital nomadism offers this freedom in spades, breaking the shackles of convention and granting the ability to design our lives on our terms.

Freedom from a fixed location is one of the most liberating aspects of the digital nomadic lifestyle. Instead of being tethered to a single geographic spot, digital nomads have the world as their backyard. They can work from a serene beach in Thailand one week and a bustling coffee shop in Berlin the next. This flexibility to roam the globe, absorbing its myriad of cultures and experiences, provides an endless variety of inspiration and perspective that few other lifestyles can match.

More than geographical freedom, digital nomadism presents the liberty to structure one's time—a departure from the rigid schedules of a traditional 9-to-5 job. This lifestyle allows individuals to set their work hours according to personal preferences and productivity cycles, thus offering a more balanced and fulfilling way of life.

Whether you're a night owl or an early bird, a marathon worker or a sprinter, digital nomadism provides the flexibility to align your work with your natural rhythms.

Another key draw of digital nomadism is the exciting prospect of adventure. The ability to delve into different cultures, explore new landscapes, and encounter diverse peoples offers a dynamic backdrop to one's life and work. Each day presents unique opportunities to learn and grow. A digital nomad's life is a heady mix of discovery, adventure, and learning that serves to enrich both their personal and professional lives.

Additionally, the revolution in technology plays a pivotal role in this lifestyle. In our current digital age, reliable internet connectivity, advanced communication tools, and the growing acceptance of remote work have blurred geographical boundaries. Work is no longer a place you go—it's what you do. The digital landscape enables you to stay connected and productive regardless of your location, transforming the world into your potential workspace.

There's also a broader societal impact of digital nomadism to consider. As nomads immerse themselves in various global communities, they contribute to the local economies and partake in cultural exchange. By doing so, they help create more interconnected and understanding societies. In essence, digital nomads become ambassadors of a form of globalization that is rooted in mutual respect and understanding, not merely commercial expansion.

Moreover, the digital nomadic lifestyle can be seen as a manifestation of the human spirit's adaptability. As we navigate through the ever-changing digital age, digital nomadism represents a resourceful and creative response to leverage technology for an enriched life experience. It's about embracing the changes, turning them to your advantage, and creating a lifestyle that is not just about surviving in the digital age, but thriving in it.

A broader perspective reveals digital nomadism to be a powerful avenue for personal growth. The experiences gained, the challenges overcome, and the insights gleaned throughout this journey foster resilience, self-reliance, and a broader understanding of the world. Each new place and culture adds another layer to the nomad's evolving worldview, ultimately leading to a richer, more nuanced understanding of both themselves and the world they inhabit.

The path to digital nomadism may appear daunting, filled with uncertainties and hurdles. Yet, the allure of this lifestyle—the promise of freedom, the anticipation of adventure, the satisfaction of personal growth, and the joy of global connectivity—is compelling enough to make the journey worthwhile. The coming chapters will delve into the practicalities and preparations for this exciting voyage, providing insights, tools, and guidance to navigate your way to a successful digital nomadic life.

Chapter 2: Deciding to **Become a Digital Nomad**: Self-Assessment and Preparations

The allure of digital nomadism is indeed potent, as we explored in the previous chapter. But, as the saying goes, every choice comes with a consequence, and thus the decision to embark on the digital nomad lifestyle should be a calculated one. This chapter will guide you through the critical process of self-assessment and preparations necessary to help you navigate this transformative decision.

The first step towards becoming a digital nomad involves a thorough self-assessment. Introspection is an invaluable tool at this juncture, one that can help you better understand your motivations, capabilities, and limitations. Why do you want to be a digital nomad? What do you hope to gain from this lifestyle? Is it the freedom, the adventure, or the potential for personal growth that attracts you the most? Remember, there is no wrong answer to these questions. The important thing is to be honest with yourself, for this clarity will guide you throughout your nomadic journey.

As well as understanding your motivations, it's crucial to assess your suitability for the lifestyle. Are you comfortable with the uncertainties that come with constant travel? Can you adapt to different cultures, customs, and languages? Do you have the discipline to manage your own schedule and meet your work commitments without supervision? If the answer to these questions is 'yes', then you're well on your way to embracing digital nomadism. However, if you find yourself hesitating, don't despair. Every trait can be honed, every challenge can be overcome with time and effort.

Once you've introspected and decided to commit to this lifestyle, it's time to get into the nitty-gritty of preparations. Being prepared is not just about drafting a bucket list of destinations; it is about developing a clear plan for your professional life, financial stability, legal responsibilities, health care, accommodation, and other such factors that are crucial for a smooth nomadic journey.

Preparing for a digital nomadic lifestyle professionally involves identifying what skills you have that can be leveraged remotely and determining the best way to monetize them. It might require you to pursue additional training or certification, or simply to rethink and reframe your existing abilities in a way that they can be applied in a remote working context. Do your research, network with other digital nomads, and explore platforms that offer remote work or freelancing opportunities in your chosen field.

Financial preparation is another critical aspect of your journey to digital nomadism. It involves careful budgeting, considering not just the travel and living expenses, but also the costs of health insurance, technology tools, co-working spaces, and unexpected contingencies. Becoming a digital nomad often means leaving a steady paycheck behind, so it's essential to establish multiple income streams and build up an emergency fund. You will also need to investigate your tax obligations as a remote worker operating from different countries.

The legalities of digital nomadism can be complex and daunting, but they cannot be ignored. From obtaining the right visas to understanding the legal implications of your remote work, these are matters that require serious attention. It's important to research thoroughly, consult with professionals if needed, and stay up to date with the changing laws and regulations.

Securing suitable accommodation is another significant consideration for any aspiring digital nomad. Today, there are numerous options available, ranging from hotels and hostels to Airbnb rentals and co-living spaces. Consider what environment will allow you to work productively while also enriching your overall travel experience.

Finally, preparing for a digital nomadic lifestyle isn't just about logistics; it's also about emotional readiness. Mental health is as important as physical health, and the nomadic lifestyle, while rewarding, can also be challenging and lonely at times. Cultivate a strong support system, develop self-care routines, and learn strategies to cope with potential isolation or culture shock.

As you delve into these preparations, it's important to remember that the transition to digital nomadism doesn't have to be abrupt. It can be gradual and phased, giving you enough time to learn, adapt, and grow into your new lifestyle. You may begin by working remotely from your home, then gradually extend your working location to different cities or countries as you become more comfortable and confident.

The decision to become a digital nomad is a significant one, shaping not just your career but your entire life. It's a decision that requires careful thought, honest self-assessment, and meticulous preparation. However, the rewards it holds—the freedom, adventure, and personal growth—are worth every ounce of effort you put in. As you stand at the threshold of this exciting journey, remember that every step you take brings you closer to the life you've always imagined. So embrace the uncertainties, equip yourself with knowledge, prepare well, and step into the world of digital nomadism with confidence and conviction. Your adventure is just beginning.

Chapter 3: **Essential Skills** for the Digital Nomad: From **Tech-Savviness** to **Adaptability**

As you're already discovering in your journey towards digital nomadism, the lifestyle demands more than just a lust for travel and a remote job. It requires a specific set of skills that will enable you to effectively manage your work and life while constantly on the move. This chapter aims to help you identify, understand, and cultivate these essential abilities, setting you on a path to success as a digital nomad.

Let's begin with tech-savviness, the bedrock of remote work. In the digital age, and more specifically in the life of a digital nomad, technology is your lifeline. It enables you to work, communicate, navigate, learn, and entertain yourself. So, it's not enough to just know how to send emails or use social media. You must develop a strong understanding of a range of technological tools and platforms related to your work, as well as those that aid travel and communication. Learning how to troubleshoot common tech issues will also save you a lot of time and frustration.

Closely linked to tech-savviness is digital security. As a digital nomad, you're likely to be working from various public networks, and your data could become vulnerable if not adequately protected. Understanding how to use Virtual Private Networks (VPNs), maintaining robust and updated antivirus software, and being knowledgeable about potential cyber threats are critical skills in safeguarding your personal and professional information.

Next up is adaptability, a trait that every successful digital nomad swears by. As you move from one place to another, you'll encounter different cultures, languages, food, climates, and ways of life. The ability to adapt quickly and comfortably to these changes can make the difference between thriving and merely surviving. Cultivating an open and curious mind, learning to embrace and respect differences, and developing problem-solving skills are all ways to boost your adaptability.

Time management is another essential skill for digital nomads. With no fixed office hours or supervision, it can be easy to procrastinate or overwork. You must learn how to create a schedule that works for you, balancing productivity with relaxation and exploration.

Understanding your work patterns, leveraging productivity tools, and mastering the art of discipline can help you manage your time effectively.

Communication skills, particularly in a digital context, are critical too. You'll often be communicating with colleagues, clients, or employers across different time zones and cultural contexts. The ability to convey your ideas clearly and concisely, understand others' perspectives, and navigate potential misunderstandings is paramount. It's also worth noting that developing a basic understanding of the local language in the places you visit can greatly enhance your overall experience.

Financial management is an indispensable skill for digital nomads. Since income streams can often be irregular, being able to manage your money effectively is crucial. This involves not just regular budgeting and tracking of expenses, but also understanding exchange rates, managing foreign transactions, and planning for future financial stability.

In addition to these, self-motivation and resilience are invaluable skills for anyone considering a nomadic lifestyle. Remote work requires a high degree of self-motivation as traditional office structures and monitoring systems are absent. Meanwhile, resilience helps you face the challenges that inevitably come with a lifestyle full of constant change.

Physical health and wellness, too, must not be overlooked. Learning to maintain a balanced diet while on the move, incorporating regular physical activity into your schedule, and knowing basic first aid procedures are all skills that will serve you well on your nomadic journey.

Lastly, networking is a skill that can open doors to exciting opportunities, help you overcome challenges, and make your nomadic journey less lonely. Mastering the art of networking involves building and maintaining relationships, both online and offline, and leveraging them effectively when required.

Each of these skills might seem overwhelming to master, but remember that every journey begins with a single step. You don't have to be an expert right away. Choose one or two skills to focus on initially, and gradually add more as you grow more comfortable. You'll be surprised how quickly you can adapt when you're motivated by the exciting prospects of digital nomadism.

Embracing the digital nomad lifestyle is not merely about crossing geographical borders. It's about expanding your horizons, growing as an individual, and learning to navigate life with a whole new set of tools. It's a journey as challenging as it is rewarding. But with the right skills in your arsenal, you're well-equipped to make the most of it. So arm yourself with knowledge, prepare well, and embark on this exciting path with confidence. The world awaits!

Chapter 4: Choosing Your Career Path: Remote Jobs and Freelancing Opportunities

Just as every traditional professional journey is unique, so is every digital nomad's career. Your work is the engine that drives your lifestyle, fueling your adventures across the globe. So, it's essential to pick a career path that not only sustains your lifestyle but also aligns with your skills, interests, and long-term goals. In this chapter, we'll explore the myriad remote jobs and freelancing opportunities available to you, and offer some tips on how to make your choice.

To start with, the digital nomad lifestyle has been made possible largely thanks to the rise of remote work. With companies across sectors embracing remote operations, especially in the wake of the COVID-19 pandemic, the opportunities for remote jobs are more abundant than ever. These range from customer service roles to programming, digital marketing to teaching, project management to consulting, and beyond.

However, the availability of remote jobs doesn't mean every role is ideal for a digital nomad. Some remote roles may require you to be online at specific hours or be available for last-minute meetings. As a digital nomad, you need to consider the time zone differences and the flexibility (or lack thereof) of your role. While it's certainly possible to work around these constraints, you must consider whether you're willing to wake up at 3 a.m. for a meeting or work late into the night to match your colleagues' time zones.

Freelancing is another option that offers a high level of flexibility, making it a popular choice among digital nomads. As a freelancer, you have more control over your work schedule, the type of work you do, and who you work for. You can choose projects that excite you and decline those that don't. However, freelancing also requires a high degree of self-motivation, discipline, and business acumen. After all, you're essentially running your own business, and that comes with additional responsibilities like finding clients, negotiating contracts, and managing your taxes.

For those with an entrepreneurial spirit, starting a location-independent business could be the path to becoming a digital nomad. This could be anything from an e-commerce store to a blog, a consulting firm, or even a digital product like an app or an online course. Starting a business requires a significant time investment upfront and may not generate income immediately. However, with determination, smart strategies, and a bit of luck, it could provide a substantial and sustainable income in the long run.

There's also the gig economy, a labor market characterized by short-term contracts or freelance work, where you can take on multiple "gigs" to create a diversified income stream. This could involve anything from graphic design to writing, virtual assisting to social media management. The gig economy offers plenty of flexibility and variety but also comes with its own challenges, like income instability and a lack of benefits.

Now, how do you choose from these options? Your choice will depend on various factors, including your skills, interests, career aspirations, and desired lifestyle. Take some time to evaluate your strengths and weaknesses, your passions, and your long-term career goals. Consider the lifestyle you want as a digital nomad: how much you wish to work, how flexible you need your schedule to be, how stable you need your income to be, and how much risk you're willing to take.

It's also worth doing some research to understand the market for your skills. Browse job boards, visit freelance platforms, and network with other digital nomads to get a sense of what's out there. This will not only help you gauge the demand for your skills but also give you an idea of the potential income you could earn.

Remember, your career path as a digital nomad doesn't have to be set in stone. It's okay to experiment, to pivot, and to evolve. You may start with a remote job, then shift to freelancing, then perhaps start a business down the line. Or you may juggle a part-time job with a few freelance gigs. The beauty of the digital nomad lifestyle is that it gives you the flexibility to design your career in a way that best suits you.

Ultimately, the goal is to find a career path that not only supports your nomadic lifestyle but also brings you satisfaction and fulfillment. After all, one of the joys of being a digital nomad is the freedom to work in a way that aligns with your lifestyle and values. So take the time to explore, to learn, and to discover the career path that truly works for you.

Chapter 5: **Financial Planning** for Digital Nomads: Budgeting, Taxes, and Income Management

Taking the leap into the digital nomad lifestyle is a thrilling decision that comes with an array of exhilarating prospects. However, amidst the allure of foreign locales and the flexibility of remote work, one crucial aspect that requires careful consideration is finances. Sound financial planning is an integral part of living a sustainable digital nomad life. In this chapter, we will delve into budgeting, handling taxes, and managing income to provide you with practical guidelines to steer your financial ship smoothly.

Let's start with budgeting, a fundamental practice that digital nomads, like everyone else, need to master. However, budgeting as a digital nomad can differ significantly from traditional budgeting. With the variation in cost of living across different countries, fluctuating income (especially for freelancers), and travel-related expenses, digital nomads need to be extra diligent and adaptive in their budgeting habits.

First and foremost, it's crucial to understand your income and expenses thoroughly. Keep track of all sources of income, whether it's from a remote job, freelancing gigs, or passive income streams. Similarly, list down all your expenses, segregating them into fixed costs (like insurance, subscriptions, etc.) and variable costs (like food, accommodation, travel, etc.). Once you have a clear picture, you can allocate your funds efficiently, ensuring you cover all necessary costs and still save for the future.

It's also important to maintain a certain level of flexibility in your budget, considering the various unforeseen expenses that might crop up in different countries. Currency fluctuations, occasional splurges, or unexpected emergencies should all be factored into your budget. A good practice is to have an "emergency fund" set aside to handle such situations without causing significant disruption to your financial plan.

Next, let's tackle the often-dreaded subject of taxes. Tax laws vary significantly worldwide, and as a digital nomad, understanding your tax obligations can be tricky. As a starting point, determine your tax residency status. Are you still considered a tax resident in your home country? Or are you classified as a non-resident? Each country has its own rules, and your status will impact your tax obligations.

You'll also need to investigate tax treaties between your home country and the countries where you'll be living. Some countries have agreements to avoid double taxation, meaning you won't be taxed twice on the same income. You should also be aware of any potential tax obligations in the countries where you're living and working. If you're staying in a country for an extended period, you may have tax responsibilities there.

Don't forget about your income sources. For instance, if you're a freelancer working for clients in different countries, you may have to deal with international taxation issues. It's recommended to consult with a tax professional who understands international tax law to ensure you're compliant and not paying more than necessary. Remember, failing to meet your tax obligations can lead to serious penalties.

Speaking of professional help, consider engaging a financial advisor, especially one familiar with the nuances of a digital nomad's life. They can help you navigate the complexities of international finances, from managing multiple currencies to optimizing your savings and investments for your mobile lifestyle. And if you're thinking about retirement (yes, even digital nomads retire!), a financial advisor can help you plan for that too.

Managing your income effectively is another crucial aspect of your financial planning. As a digital nomad, especially if you're a freelancer or run your own business, your income might be irregular. Therefore, it's essential to manage your funds so that you can cover lean periods without stress. This might mean setting aside a portion of your income during good months to cover expenses during slower periods. It could also mean diversifying your income sources to create more stability.

One effective strategy to manage your income is to automate your finances as much as possible.

Setting up automatic transfers to your savings account or automatic bill payments can ensure that you're consistently saving and keeping up with your financial obligations, even when you're caught up in the thrill of exploring a new city or meeting deadlines for work.

Being a digital nomad means embracing a degree of uncertainty – it's part of the adventure. But when it comes to your finances, having a solid plan can provide stability amidst the unknowns. With careful budgeting, a thorough understanding of your tax obligations, and effective income management, you can ensure your financial health while living the nomadic life you've dreamed of. It's about striking the right balance between the freedom of the lifestyle and the responsibility it entails. And once you find this balance, the world truly is your oyster.

Chapter 6: Destination Decisions: Picking the **Right Countries** and **Cities**

One of the most exciting aspects of the digital nomad lifestyle is the freedom to choose your workplace. Gone are the days when you were tied to a desk in a dull, grey office. Now, your office could be a beachfront café in Bali, a bustling co-working space in Berlin, or a serene park in Kyoto. The world is your oyster, but this array of choices brings forth the question: where should you go?

Choosing the right destination is more than just picking a place on the map. It's about finding locations that align with your lifestyle, work needs, budget, and personal preferences. In this chapter, we explore the process of making destination decisions and provide you with insights to help you pick the right countries and cities for your digital nomad journey.

Firstly, let's consider the aspect of lifestyle. What are your preferences? Do you enjoy the hustle and bustle of big cities, or do you prefer quiet towns? Are you an outdoors person who enjoys nature and adventure sports, or do you prefer cultural activities like museum visits and historical tours? Your destination should align with these preferences to ensure that you enjoy your time off work. For instance, if you're a beach lover, places like Bali, the Canary Islands, or Thailand could be excellent choices.

Work needs are another crucial consideration. Your destination should support your work in terms of resources and infrastructure. For instance, if you're a software developer or a graphic designer, you need robust internet connectivity and a peaceful place to work. Check for locations that have reliable internet and good co-working spaces. Countries with a digital nomad-friendly ecosystem, such as Estonia, which even offers a digital nomad visa, could be great options.

Time zones can also be a significant factor, especially if you're required to collaborate with a team or cater to clients in a particular region. For example, if most of your clients are in the US, choosing a destination with a significantly different time zone, like Australia, might pose challenges.

Your budget plays an essential role in your decision-making process. The cost of living varies significantly across different countries. While Southeast Asian countries like Thailand or Vietnam can be very affordable, living in European cities like London or Paris can be considerably more expensive. It's important to choose a destination that fits well within your budget. Take into account not just the living costs, but also the cost of activities you enjoy, health insurance costs, flight costs, and so on.

Safety is another critical consideration. As attractive as a destination may be, it's essential that it's safe for foreigners. Look into the crime rates, the political situation, and any other factors that might affect your safety. It's also worth considering health safety, especially in the context of recent global events like the COVID-19 pandemic.

Next, let's talk about visas. The visa policies of a country can significantly affect your stay duration and work legality. Some countries offer digital nomad visas that allow foreigners to stay and work legally for a certain period. Others might have strict policies that limit your stay or work possibilities. Thoroughly research the visa requirements and policies of your intended destination before making a decision.

Language can also play a role in your decision. While English is commonly spoken in many parts of the world, there are places where not knowing the local language can be a hurdle. If you're open to learning a new language, this could be a fascinating aspect of your digital nomad journey. However, if you prefer to stick to English, destinations like Malta, the Philippines, or any English-speaking country could be preferable.

Lastly, consider the community aspect. Being a digital nomad doesn't mean you have to be alone. Many places around the world have vibrant digital nomad communities that you can be a part of. These communities can be a great source of companionship, networking, and support. Locations like Chiang Mai, Medellín, or Lisbon are known for their thriving digital nomad communities.

Choosing your destination is a thrilling part of your digital nomad journey. It's like picking a new home, one that aligns with your professional needs and personal desires. Every place you choose will become a chapter in your life's story, a backdrop against which you'll create memories, achieve milestones, and experience growth. Therefore, take your time, do your research, and listen to your instincts. And always remember, the beauty of being a digital nomad is that if you don't like a place, you can always move to the next one. It's your journey, and you're in the driver's seat.

Chapter 7: Navigating Visa and **Legal** **Matters**: A Guide for the Global Worker

Embracing the digital nomad lifestyle is an adventure that excites and challenges in equal measure. The idea of working from exotic locations, experiencing diverse cultures, and enjoying a flexible schedule is understandably alluring. However, while the romantic notion of setting up your portable office in a hammock strung between palm trees on a remote beach is tantalizing, it's essential not to forget the very real legal considerations that come with this lifestyle. In this chapter, we will delve into the critical area of visas and legal matters that every digital nomad should understand.

For most digital nomads, the term 'visa' will become an essential part of their lexicon. Whether you wish to work from a beach in Bali or a café in Copenhagen, you must have the appropriate visa that allows you entry and a legal stay in your destination country. Let's explore the myriad of visa options available and the legal considerations surrounding them.

Traditionally, the most common types of visas digital nomads have used are tourist visas. However, using a tourist visa to work in a country can pose legal issues, as these visas typically do not permit foreign nationals to engage in employment within the host country. Even if the work is carried out remotely for a non-local company, it can sometimes still be considered as a breach of visa conditions.

To address this issue, some countries have started introducing digital nomad or remote work visas.

These are specially designed for individuals who wish to work remotely for an overseas employer or their own business while residing in a different country. For instance, Estonia's Digital Nomad Visa and Barbados' 12-month Barbados Welcome Stamp are designed to enable remote workers and their families to live in these countries while continuing to work remotely.

Obtaining a digital nomad visa is usually a clear and straightforward process, but it does require an application process and some documentation. Requirements typically include proof of employment or business ownership, evidence of sufficient income, and sometimes health insurance coverage. As these types of visas are relatively new, the rules and regulations can vary significantly between countries. It's crucial to check the latest information on the official government websites or consult with a legal expert familiar with immigration law.

There are also other types of visas that digital nomads may use, such as business or student visas, although these come with their own sets of restrictions and conditions. A business visa generally allows individuals to do business, but not take up employment, while a student visa, usually given to those pursuing education in the host country, often has stipulations about the hours one can work.

Aside from visas, there are other legal matters that digital nomads need to be aware of. Taxation is a major one. The tax laws that apply to digital nomads can be complex and vary greatly depending on the countries involved. Generally, you would need to consider both the tax laws of your home country and the country where you are staying. Some countries have tax treaties in place to prevent double taxation, but understanding what taxes you're liable for can be complicated and may require the assistance of a tax professional.

Data protection and privacy laws are another area that digital nomads must consider. If your work involves handling personal data, especially from clients or customers, you need to be aware of the data protection laws in your home country, your host country, and potentially also the countries of your clients or customers.

Intellectual property laws can also be a concern for those who create content or products while abroad. Different countries have varying laws and protections regarding copyright, patents, trademarks, and other intellectual property rights.

In addition, digital nomads should be aware of any local laws and customs in their host country. These could relate to anything from dress codes and local etiquette to more serious legal matters like drug laws. Respect for local culture and laws is not just a legal necessity, but also crucial to being a responsible and respectful visitor.

Legal matters can sometimes seem daunting, and it might be tempting to take shortcuts or make assumptions based on anecdotal advice from other digital nomads. However, failing to respect and adhere to the appropriate laws and regulations can lead to serious consequences, ranging from fines and deportation to being barred from entering certain countries in the future.

Being a successful digital nomad involves balancing the freedom and flexibility of this lifestyle with a keen understanding and respect for the laws of the countries you choose to reside in. By staying informed and taking the necessary steps to comply with these laws, you can ensure a smooth and stress-free digital nomad journey.

Chapter 8: **Accommodations** and Living Arrangements: From **Co-Living Spaces** to **Airbnb**

While the notion of a digital nomad life is often seen through the prism of independence and flexibility, a significant aspect of this lifestyle involves the question of where to stay. The options for digital nomad accommodations are vast and can range from traditional rentals and hotel stays to modern co-living spaces and short-term lodging platforms like Airbnb. This chapter offers a comprehensive look into these possibilities and provides insights into the nuances involved in selecting the best living arrangement as a digital nomad.

Firstly, let's explore the concept of co-living spaces. This recent trend in the housing market offers a mix of private and shared spaces that create an environment conducive to both work and social interactions. Co-living spaces are typically furnished and equipped with amenities like high-speed internet, communal workspaces, and often recreational facilities such as fitness centers or game rooms. These spaces provide an excellent opportunity for digital nomads to meet like-minded individuals and form communities, making them especially appealing for solo travelers.

Services like Outsite, Selina, and Roam offer a network of co-living spaces in various locations around the world. Their focus on catering to the needs of remote workers makes them a reliable choice for many digital nomads. They often offer flexible booking options, from a few days to several months, making it easier for nomads to plan their stays around their travel plans.

The allure of co-living spaces, however, may not appeal to everyone. For those seeking more privacy or specific types of accommodation, Airbnb can offer a vast array of options. From entire apartments to unique stays like treehouses or boats, Airbnb gives digital nomads the ability to tailor their living arrangements to their preferences. Moreover, many Airbnb hosts are familiar with the needs of digital nomads, ensuring that their listings are equipped with stable Wi-Fi and work-friendly spaces.

Another significant advantage of using Airbnb is the extensive reach of the platform. Whether you're planning to live in a bustling city, a quiet countryside, or even a remote island, chances are, you can find an Airbnb there. While long-term stays on Airbnb can sometimes be pricey, many hosts offer substantial discounts for stays of a month or longer. In addition, the rating and review system on the platform can provide a clear idea of what to expect from the accommodation.

Alternatively, traditional apartment or house rentals can be a viable option, especially for longer stays or for those traveling with families or pets. Websites like Craigslist, Rightmove, or country-specific real estate platforms can be valuable resources for finding long-term rentals. This type of accommodation often requires a more considerable amount of paperwork and a longer-term commitment than co-living spaces or Airbnb, but it can provide a more 'home-like' environment and is usually more cost-effective for long-term stays.

When looking at traditional rentals, it's also important to consider the location and local amenities. Proximity to supermarkets, public transport, hospitals, and recreational areas can significantly affect your quality of life. Using Google Maps or local forums can provide insight into the neighborhood and what it has to offer.

For those who prefer to stay on the move, options like van living or house-sitting might be appealing. Living in a van or an RV allows for a high level of mobility and can be a great way to explore a country at your own pace. However, it requires a substantial upfront investment and ongoing maintenance. Similarly, house-sitting, where you look after someone's home while they're away, can provide free accommodation and a chance to live like a local, but it typically requires references and a level of responsibility towards the property and any pets in the home.

In each of these living arrangements, there are a few key factors that digital nomads must consider. Reliable internet is vital for remote work, and it should be one of the first things you check. Secondly, a comfortable workspace is essential. While a kitchen table might be sufficient for some, others might require a proper desk or an ergonomic chair. Additionally, consider the local time zone and how it aligns with your work hours, particularly if you need to coordinate with colleagues or clients in different parts of the world.

Security is another crucial aspect to keep in mind. Make sure that your living arrangement has safe storage for your belongings, especially expensive items like laptops or cameras. Travel insurance that covers your gear can be a lifesaver in case of theft or damage.

Lastly, your accommodation should be a place where you feel comfortable and at ease. Since the pandemic, the line between work and home has blurred for many people, and it's crucial to create a living space that aids productivity but also allows you to relax and unwind.

Choosing the right accommodation as a digital nomad depends on individual preferences, work needs, and lifestyle. Whether you opt for the community-oriented environment of a co-living space, the flexibility of Airbnb, or the stability of a traditional rental, the most important thing is to make an informed decision that best supports your needs as a digital nomad. By doing so, you'll be creating a home-away-from-home that serves not only as a place to work but also a haven to rest, rejuvenate, and immerse yourself in the local culture.

Chapter 9: **Health** and **Wellness** on the Road: **Insurance**, **Fitness**, and Self-Care

Maintaining a healthy lifestyle is vital for everyone, but when it comes to the digital nomad lifestyle, the significance of health and wellness often takes on a new meaning. This chapter delves into the critical facets of health and wellness for digital nomads, ranging from securing the right health insurance to ensuring consistent physical fitness and prioritizing self-care, all within the context of a life that is perpetually on the move.

To start with, health insurance is one of the fundamental aspects of a digital nomad's life. Due to the nomadic nature of their lifestyle, traditional health insurance policies might not always offer the coverage required when living and working abroad. Hence, it becomes imperative for digital nomads to find a suitable international health insurance plan that ensures coverage across different countries.

Several insurance providers specialize in offering international health insurance plans that cater to the specific needs of digital nomads. Companies like SafetyWing, World Nomads, and Cigna Global provide flexible and comprehensive coverage that includes everything from routine checkups and emergency treatments to medical evacuation. Additionally, it is essential to ensure that your policy covers treatment for COVID-19, given the ongoing pandemic situation worldwide.

While choosing a health insurance plan, consider factors like the duration of coverage, geographical limits, deductibles, policy exclusions, and, importantly, the claim process. Also, keep in mind that health insurance does not generally cover pre-existing conditions, so if you have any, look for policies that offer coverage for such situations.

Once the insurance aspects are covered, the next crucial area of concern is maintaining physical health. A digital nomad lifestyle, while exciting, often involves long hours of work coupled with travel, which might lead to neglecting physical fitness. Incorporating regular physical activity into your routine can not only keep you fit but also greatly contribute to your mental wellbeing.

With traditional gyms and fitness centers not always being a viable option due to constant travel, digital nomads have to get creative with their fitness routines. Here are a few suggestions:

1. **Bodyweight Exercises:** These are exercises that use your own body weight as resistance and can be performed anywhere, anytime. Push-ups, squats, lunges, and planks are some examples.

There are numerous online resources and apps that provide guided bodyweight workout routines suitable for all fitness levels.

2. Yoga or Pilates: Both are excellent for flexibility, strength, and balance, and require minimal equipment – just a yoga mat. Online platforms like YouTube or fitness apps offer a plethora of guided routines that you can follow.

3. Running or Cycling: If you're in a location that's conducive to outdoor activities, running or cycling can be great ways to stay fit while also exploring your surroundings.

4. Portable Fitness Equipment: Resistance bands, skipping ropes, or portable suspension trainers can be easily packed in your luggage and help add variety to your workouts.

Alongside physical health, mental wellness is a cornerstone of a digital nomad's wellbeing. The novelty and excitement of travel and working from exotic locations can sometimes obscure the potential stressors and mental health challenges that can arise. Loneliness, culture shock, work-related stress, or simply being far from your support network can take a toll on your mental health.

Practices such as meditation and mindfulness can be powerful tools in maintaining mental balance. Apps like Headspace or Calm provide guided meditations and mindfulness exercises that can help manage stress and anxiety. Similarly, keeping a journal can be a therapeutic way of expressing and processing your experiences and emotions.

Additionally, there are online therapy platforms, such as BetterHelp or Talkspace, which offer virtual counseling services. These can be immensely helpful, especially given the remote nature of a digital nomad's life.

Nutrition is another critical aspect of health that can be challenging for digital nomads. Moving between countries with different cuisines can make it hard to maintain a consistent and balanced diet. While it's essential to enjoy and explore the local cuisine, it's equally important to ensure you're getting a balanced intake of nutrients. Planning meals, including a variety of local fruits and vegetables in your diet, staying hydrated, and limiting the intake of fast food can contribute to better nutrition.

Moreover, rest and relaxation should not be overlooked. Irregular schedules and crossing time zones can disrupt sleep patterns, leading to fatigue and reduced productivity. Prioritizing quality sleep and taking time out to relax and engage in non-work-related activities are essential for overall health and wellbeing.

In the realm of digital nomadism, health and wellness stretch beyond mere freedom from illness. It encompasses physical fitness, mental wellbeing, dietary health, rest, relaxation, and overall self-care. While the dynamic nature of this lifestyle might present certain challenges in maintaining consistent health and wellness practices, the solutions are plentiful and adaptable, much like the digital nomad life itself. It's all about finding what works best for you, making health a priority, and remembering that it's your wellbeing that fuels this adventurous lifestyle.

Chapter 10: Building Your Digital Toolbox: Essential Software and Apps for Remote Work

As the name implies, the lifestyle of a digital nomad is heavily reliant on digital tools. These tools serve as the bedrock of the digital nomad's existence, helping to bridge the gap between work and travel. Whether it's managing tasks, staying connected with clients and colleagues, or ensuring seamless financial transactions, the right digital toolbox can significantly enhance a digital nomad's productivity, communication, and overall work efficiency.

This chapter aims to guide you in building your own digital toolbox, focusing on essential software and apps that cater to the diverse needs of remote work and travel.

Project Management and Productivity Tools

Project management and productivity tools are an absolute necessity to stay organized and efficient, especially when working on multiple projects simultaneously or as part of a remote team. These tools provide a centralized platform to manage tasks, track progress, and facilitate collaboration.

1. Asana: Asana is a versatile project management tool that allows you to create and assign tasks, set deadlines, and share files. It's ideal for managing complex projects and collaborating with teams.

2. Trello: Trello is another project management tool that uses a board-and-card system to manage tasks. It's visually appealing and straightforward, making it suitable for both individuals and teams.

3. Notion: Notion serves as an all-in-one workspace where you can write, plan, collaborate, and organize. It's known for its flexible and customizable interface.

4. Evernote: Evernote is an excellent tool for note-taking, organizing, task management, and archiving. It allows you to capture and prioritize ideas, projects, and to-do lists.

Communication Tools

Keeping open lines of communication is critical when working remotely. Here, the focus is on tools that facilitate communication and collaboration with clients and teams dispersed across different time zones.

1. Slack: Slack is a popular messaging app for teams that facilitates communication through text, voice, and video. It allows for the creation of different channels for separate projects or departments.

2. Zoom: Zoom is a video conferencing tool that allows for meetings, webinars, and even phone calls. It's become a staple in the remote work setup due to its reliability and ease of use.

3. Microsoft Teams: Part of the Microsoft 365 suite, Teams provides a hub for teamwork where you can chat, meet, call, and collaborate all in one place.

Financial Tools

As a digital nomad, managing finances, sending invoices, and tracking expenses can be a challenge. Fortunately, there are numerous apps designed to handle these tasks efficiently.

1. PayPal: PayPal is a widely accepted platform for online money transfers. It's useful for invoicing clients, making purchases, and receiving payments.

2. TransferWise (now Wise): Wise is ideal for international money transfers, offering better exchange rates and lower fees than most traditional banks.

3. Expensify: Expensify simplifies the process of expense management. It's ideal for tracking receipts and managing expenses on the go.

Cloud Storage and File Sharing

Cloud storage and file sharing services are essential for accessing work files across different devices and sharing them with clients or team members.

1. **Google Drive**: Google Drive offers free cloud storage and has seamless integration with Google Workspace apps like Google Docs, Sheets, and Slides.

2. **Dropbox**: Dropbox is another popular choice for cloud storage and file sharing. It's simple, easy to use, and has a feature that allows for syncing specific folders on your computer.

3. **OneDrive**: Part of the Microsoft 365 suite, OneDrive integrates well with Microsoft apps and offers substantial storage space.

Time Management and Scheduling

When living as a digital nomad, it's important to keep track of time across different time zones. Scheduling tools can also streamline the process of setting up meetings or managing your calendar.

1. World Time Buddy: This is a convenient world clock, a time zone converter, and an online meeting scheduler. It's one of the best online productivity tools for those often finding themselves traveling, especially through different time zones.

2. Google Calendar: Google's scheduling calendar service enables you to create and edit events. Reminders can be enabled for events, with options available for type and time.

3. Calendly: Calendly helps schedule meetings without the back-and-forth emails. It allows people to schedule meetings with you based on your availability.

VPN Services

A VPN, or Virtual Private Network, ensures a secure internet connection that protects your privacy and data, particularly important when accessing the internet from public Wi-Fi networks.

1. **NordVPN**: Known for its advanced security, internet freedom, and complete privacy, NordVPN is a solid choice for digital nomads.

2. **ExpressVPN**: ExpressVPN is another highly-rated option that offers fast speeds, reliability, and a vast network of servers around the world.

While this is not an exhaustive list, these tools constitute a fundamental part of most digital nomads' toolboxes. They cater to the diverse needs of remote work, from task management and communication to financial transactions and internet security. The key is to identify what tools work best for you depending on your specific needs, work style, and

nature of work. Building an effective digital toolbox can significantly improve your productivity and efficiency, making the digital nomad lifestyle smoother and more manageable.

Chapter 11: Staying Connected: Managing **Relationships** and Networking **While Abroad**

The lifestyle of a digital nomad brings with it a unique set of challenges, not the least of which is staying connected. This connection isn't limited to maintaining strong WiFi for work purposes; it extends to nurturing relationships and networking while on the road. This chapter delves into how digital nomads can effectively manage their relationships, both personal and professional, and utilize networking opportunities while living a nomadic lifestyle.

Maintaining Personal Relationships

Leaving behind a familiar life to become a digital nomad often means leaving behind friends and family. While physical distance can put a strain on these relationships, today's technology offers various ways to stay in touch and maintain close ties, no matter where in the world you might be.

1. Scheduled Calls and Virtual Hangouts: Regular communication is key to maintaining relationships. Schedule regular calls or virtual hangouts using video conferencing tools like Skype, Zoom, or Google Meet. Making these virtual meet-ups a regular part of your routine can help you stay connected with your loved ones.

2. Social Media and Messaging Apps: Platforms like Facebook, Instagram, and WhatsApp make sharing experiences easy. Posting updates and photos, instant messaging, or sharing snippets of your life on Instagram Stories can help you stay in the loop with your friends' and family's lives and vice versa.

3. Virtual Reality (VR) Gatherings: Virtual Reality technology, such as Oculus, can provide a sense of "being there" far better than regular video calls. VR chat rooms allow you to hang out with friends and family in a more immersive way.

4. Sending Letters or Postcards: This may seem old-fashioned in the digital era, but sending postcards from your travels or handwritten letters can be a heartwarming way to let someone know you're thinking of them.

Building and Maintaining Professional Relationships

For digital nomads, establishing and nurturing professional relationships can provide a multitude of benefits, including new work opportunities, collaboration, learning, and personal growth.

1. Join Local Networking Events: Most cities have networking events or meet-ups related to various professional fields. Platforms like Meetup.com or Eventbrite can be useful to find such events.

2. Co-working Spaces: These places are not just for working; they are also hubs for meeting other digital nomads, freelancers, and professionals. Participating in events organized by the co-working space can also open opportunities for collaboration or learning.

3. Professional Networking Platforms: LinkedIn is a powerful tool for maintaining professional relationships and networking. Regularly updating your profile, posting updates, participating in discussions, and reaching out to new connections can help keep your professional network strong.

4. Alumni Networks: If you've attended a college or university, leverage your alumni network. Many institutions have global alumni associations, which can be an excellent way to connect with professionals in different parts of the world.

5. Industry Conferences and Seminars: Although you're on the move, don't underestimate the value of industry conferences and seminars. These events can be hotspots for networking and staying up-to-date with your field.

Creating New Relationships on the Road

One of the most exciting aspects of being a digital nomad is the opportunity to meet new people from diverse backgrounds. Forming new relationships on the road can lead to lifelong friendships and enrich your travel experience.

1. **Stay Socially Active:** Participate in local events, cultural activities, or community gatherings. This can be an effective way to meet locals and other travelers.

2. **Language Exchange Meet-ups:** If you're in a country where a different language is spoken, join language exchange meet-ups. It's a fantastic way to learn the local language and make new friends.

3. **Group Tours or Classes:** Participate in group activities, like city tours, cooking classes, or even yoga sessions. Such activities are great ice-breakers and offer a shared experience to bond over.

4. Digital Nomad Communities: There are numerous online and offline communities for digital nomads. Join these communities for advice, companionship, or even finding travel partners. Examples include Nomad List, Couchsurfing, or the Digital Nomad Reddit community.

Living as a digital nomad doesn't mean you have to disconnect from your existing relationships or miss out on creating new ones. In fact, it can be an opportunity to build a diverse and global network. The key lies in making an effort to maintain these connections and being open to forming new ones.

Chapter 12: Dealing with **Challenges**: Overcoming **Loneliness**, **Burnout**, and Culture Shock

Embracing the digital nomad lifestyle can offer unprecedented freedom, adventure, and opportunities for personal growth. However, this way of living also comes with unique challenges. In this chapter, we will discuss strategies to deal with some of the most common issues faced by digital nomads: loneliness, burnout, and culture shock.

1. Overcoming Loneliness

The freedom to travel and work from anywhere can sometimes lead to a sense of isolation and loneliness. Here are some strategies to help you combat these feelings:

* **Find Your Tribe:** Look for local meetups, events, or co-working spaces where you can connect with like-minded individuals. There are many online communities and forums for digital nomads where you can find support and advice, or even plan meetups.

* **Keep Regular Contact With Loved Ones:** Use video call platforms to maintain regular contact with friends and family back home.

* **Engage in Community Activities:** Join local clubs or groups based on your interests. This could be language exchange groups, fitness classes, or volunteer programs.

* **Adopt a Pet:** If your lifestyle permits, consider adopting a pet. Having a companion can reduce feelings of loneliness.

2. Avoiding Burnout

The blurring of boundaries between work and personal life can often lead to burnout for digital nomads. Here are some tips to maintain a healthy work-life balance and prevent burnout:

* **Maintain Regular Work Hours**: Just as you would in a traditional work setting, set specific work hours and stick to them. Make sure to separate your working time from your personal time.

* **Take Regular Breaks**: Ensure you take short breaks during your workday. Use this time to stretch, take a walk, meditate, or engage in any non-work activity that you enjoy.

* **Prioritize Your Health**: Regular exercise, a healthy diet, and sufficient sleep are crucial for

preventing burnout. Try to incorporate these into your daily routine.

* **Take Time Off**: Just because you're living in a beautiful location doesn't mean you're on a perpetual vacation. Ensure you take days off work to relax and explore.

3. Dealing With Culture Shock

Moving to a new country can bring about a sense of disorientation known as culture shock. Here's how you can deal with it:

* **Learn About the Culture Before You Arrive**: Before you move to a new country, spend time researching its culture, traditions, and etiquette. Understanding these can help you feel more comfortable when you arrive.

* **Learn the Local Language**: Knowing the local language, even just a few basic phrases, can greatly enhance your experience and interactions with locals.

* **Be Open and Adaptable**: Keep an open mind and be prepared to adapt to new ways of doing things. Remember, one of the reasons you chose this lifestyle is to experience and learn from different cultures.

* **Connect with Other Expats**: Connecting with other expats or digital nomads can provide comfort and practical advice, as they're likely to have had similar experiences.

No lifestyle is without its challenges, and being a digital nomad is no exception. While loneliness, burnout, and culture shock are common issues faced by many digital nomads, they can be managed and overcome with the right strategies and mindset. By dealing with these challenges effectively, you can ensure that your experience as a digital nomad is both personally and professionally rewarding.

Chapter 13: The Digital Nomad Lifestyle: **Daily Routines** and **Work-Life Balance**

Living the digital nomad lifestyle is about more than just traveling and working; it's about creating a balanced life that promotes productivity, personal growth, and wellness. Maintaining a daily routine and achieving work-life balance is crucial, and in this chapter, we'll delve into various strategies to help you craft a fulfilling and sustainable lifestyle.

1. Establishing a Routine

The freedom to work from anywhere might make it tempting to abandon routine, but maintaining a semblance of structure is vital for productivity and mental health. Here's how to go about it:

* **Set Regular Work Hours**: Consider the time zones you're working with, your personal productivity patterns, and your leisure plans. It's okay to adjust as needed, but try to stick to a consistent schedule.

* **Plan Your Work**: Make a daily or weekly to-do list. Define your objectives, prioritize tasks, and set clear deadlines. This can help you stay organized and avoid feeling overwhelmed.

* **Reserve Time for Leisure**: Don't let work consume your entire day. Plan time for

sightseeing, hobbies, rest, exercise, socializing, and other non-work activities.

* **Stick to a Sleep Schedule:** Despite changing time zones, aim for a consistent sleep schedule to ensure you're well-rested. Good sleep is crucial for cognitive functions and overall health.

2. Work-Life Balance

Achieving a healthy work-life balance as a digital nomad can be challenging but is crucial for maintaining your health and happiness. Here are some strategies:

* **Create Physical Work-Life Boundaries:** If possible, have a separate workspace in your accommodation. Avoid working from your bed or areas associated with relaxation.

* **Limit Work Communications**: Set boundaries with clients or colleagues to ensure you're not expected to be available 24/7. Consider turning off notifications during your non-work hours.

* **Take Regular Breaks and Days Off**: Remember, it's essential to give yourself regular breaks and days off. Explore, unwind, recharge - this is part of the joy of being a digital nomad!

* **Prioritize Self-Care**: Regular exercise, healthy meals, mindfulness activities, hobbies - they all contribute to a balanced life. Prioritize them just as you would prioritize work.

3. Navigating Time Zone Differences

One specific challenge digital nomads face is dealing with different time zones. Here's how you can manage this:

* **Use Tools to Track Time Zones**: Use digital tools and apps that help you track and manage different time zones. This can help avoid scheduling mishaps.

* **Communicate Your Availability**: Let your clients, colleagues, or managers know your availability in their time zone. Set expectations and communicate any changes to your schedule when you move to a new time zone.

* **Balance Your Schedule**: When working across different time zones, make sure your schedule allows for adequate sleep and leisure time.

Living as a digital nomad doesn't mean abandoning structure and routine. A well-designed daily routine and balanced lifestyle can lead to improved productivity, health, and satisfaction. By successfully managing your work, leisure, and personal care, you can fully enjoy the benefits of the digital nomad lifestyle, turning this unique experience into a sustainable way of living.

Chapter 14: Nurturing **Personal Growth**: Learning from Your Experiences Abroad

One of the greatest benefits of living the digital nomad lifestyle is the endless opportunities for personal growth. New experiences, cultures, people, and environments provide fertile ground for expanding your horizons and learning more about yourself and the world. This chapter explores how to nurture personal growth during your digital nomad journey.

1. Openness to New Experiences

To fully reap the benefits of your nomadic lifestyle, it's important to approach your experiences with an open mind. Here are some tips on how to do this:

* **Try New Things**: Whether it's local food, new hobbies, or different forms of entertainment, take advantage of the opportunities that come your way.

* **Interact with Locals**: Engage with locals to gain a more authentic experience of the places you visit. You can learn about local traditions, language, and way of life.

* **Volunteer or Participate in Local Activities:** This not only contributes to your personal growth but can also create positive impacts within the communities you visit.

2. Embracing Cultural Diversity

As a digital nomad, you'll be exposed to diverse cultures. Embracing this diversity can significantly enhance your personal growth.

* **Learn the Language**: Even basic knowledge of the local language can go a long way in understanding a culture. Language learning apps can be a great starting point.

* **Respect Cultural Norms**: Research and respect local traditions and customs. This not only shows respect to the locals but can also prevent cultural misunderstandings.

* **Participate in Cultural Activities**: Joining local festivals, events, or community activities can be a great way to immerse yourself in the culture.

3. Learning from Challenges

The digital nomad lifestyle isn't always smooth sailing. Challenges and setbacks can be learning opportunities.

* **Stay Resilient**: Developing resilience helps you recover from setbacks and adapt to change, essential skills for any digital nomad.

* **Learn to Solve Problems**: Travel challenges require innovative solutions. Over time, this can improve your problem-solving skills.

* **Develop Emotional Intelligence**: Dealing with stressful situations and cultural differences can enhance your emotional intelligence, increasing your empathy and understanding of others.

4. Continuous Education and Skill Development

Living as a digital nomad doesn't mean putting your education or professional development on hold. Here are some ways to keep learning and growing:

* **Online Courses and Webinars**: There are plenty of online resources available to help you learn new skills or deepen your existing ones. Platforms like Coursera, Udemy, or LinkedIn Learning offer courses on various topics.

* **Networking**: Regularly communicate with other digital nomads or professionals in your field. They can provide fresh perspectives, advice, and opportunities for collaboration.

* **Reading**: Keep learning about the countries you visit, industry trends, new tools and technologies, and more. Reading expands your knowledge and understanding of the world.

Personal growth is an ongoing journey, and as a digital nomad, your experiences abroad offer abundant opportunities for learning and development. By maintaining an open mind, embracing cultural diversity, learning from challenges, and prioritizing continuous education, you can make the most of your digital nomad journey. Remember, every experience, good or bad, contributes to your growth. By consciously seeking to learn from these experiences, you're investing in a valuable asset: yourself.

Chapter 15: The Future of Digital Nomadism: Sustainability and Long-Term Perspectives

As we wrap up this comprehensive guide on digital nomadism, it's fitting to take a glimpse into the future. The concept of living and working remotely has changed the face of employment and lifestyle design, but what's next for this lifestyle trend? In this chapter, we'll discuss the sustainability of digital nomadism and offer some long-term perspectives.

1. Evolving Work Culture and Digital Nomadism

Work culture is changing globally, and the rise of remote work has been instrumental in this shift. Here, we'll examine how these changes could influence the future of digital nomadism.

* **Greater Adoption of Remote Work:** More companies are embracing remote work arrangements, allowing their employees to work from anywhere. As businesses recognize the benefits of remote work, such as reduced overhead costs and increased employee

satisfaction, this trend is likely to continue, fostering the growth of digital nomadism.

* **Co-Working and Co-Living Spaces**: The demand for co-working and co-living spaces has risen with the growth of digital nomadism. These spaces offer networking opportunities and community experiences, making them an appealing choice for digital nomads. The future might see a surge in these spaces, especially in popular digital nomad cities.

* **Technology Advancements**: As technology continues to evolve, so will the tools that facilitate remote work. From more reliable and widespread internet connectivity to advancements in communication tools and digital security, the future of technology holds immense potential for simplifying the digital nomad lifestyle.

2. Sustainability of Digital Nomadism

As digital nomadism continues to grow, considerations around its sustainability come to the fore. Here are some aspects to consider:

* **Environmental Impact**: Travel is an integral part of digital nomadism, and it has an environmental cost. Conscious travel choices, such as slow travel, can reduce this impact. Moreover, digital nomads typically consume less energy than traditional office-based employees, which is a positive aspect.

* **Economic Impact on Local Communities**: Digital nomads contribute to the local economy of the places they visit by using local services and businesses. However, it's essential for nomads to be mindful of their impact and ensure they are contributing positively to the local economy without causing inflation or over-tourism.

3. Long-Term Perspectives on Digital Nomadism

Looking at long-term perspectives, one might wonder whether it's feasible to maintain a digital nomad lifestyle indefinitely. Here are a few things to think about:

* **Potential for Regulation:** As more people embrace the digital nomad lifestyle, governments may need to introduce specific regulations and visa categories for them, which can influence the feasibility and attractiveness of the lifestyle in various countries.

* **Personal Considerations:** On a personal level, long-term digital nomadism can be influenced by factors such as family planning, the desire for a permanent base, or changes in one's career. Regular reassessment of one's needs and lifestyle choices is crucial.

* **Retirement Planning:** Long-term financial planning and retirement can be more complex for digital nomads, who often don't have traditional employment benefits. However, with proper planning and financial management, it's possible to navigate these complexities.

The future of digital nomadism is bright, with evolving work cultures increasingly accommodating this lifestyle and technological advancements simplifying it. However, like any lifestyle choice, it should be pursued mindfully, considering the potential impacts on oneself, local communities, and the environment. As the landscape of work continues to shift, digital nomadism offers an alternative path that can bring both professional and personal rewards. As we navigate this promising yet uncertain future, adaptability, continuous learning, and awareness remain key traits for any successful digital nomad.